# Paisley Pig and Friends

## A Multicultural ABC

## Willow Bascom

PublishingWorks, Inc.
2010

PublishingWorks, Inc.
151 Epping Road
Exeter, NH 03833
603-778-9883

For Sales and Orders:
1-800-738-6603 or 603-772-7200
www.PublishingWorks.com

LCCN: 2009925821
ISBN-13: 978-1-935557-54-8

Manufactured by Friesens Corp., Altona, MB Canada, April 2010.

# Paisley Pig and Friends

## A Multicultural ABC

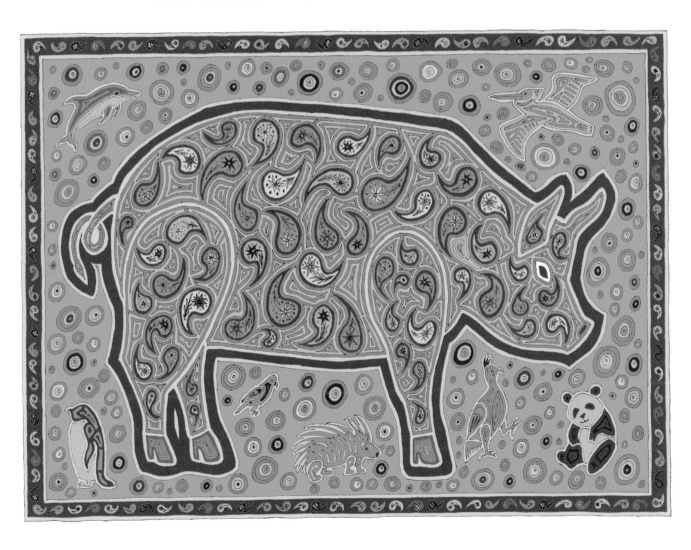

Dedicated to:

my husband
Terry - who recognized the beginning and
kept me going till the end.

our children
Stefanie - her love of world cultures,
Christopher - remember drawing side by side?
Phillip - who always wanted the facts.

my friends
Hope, Polly, Wendy, Barbara, Bea, Anne,
Karin, Jim and Bonnie, Naomi,
and the other Willow.

# Aa Argyle Alligators

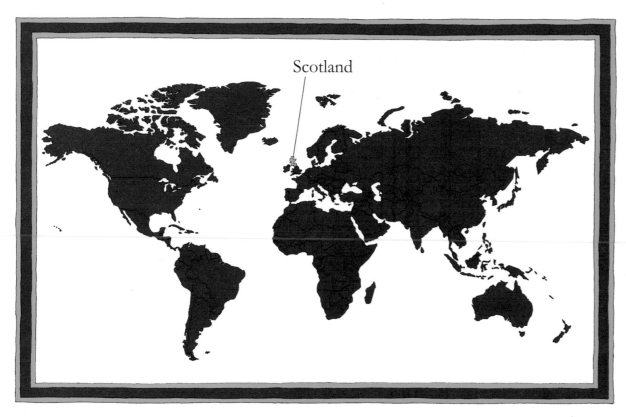

Scotland

Argyle was created as a pattern for knitting. It is made of solid and outlined diamonds. Argyle socks, sweaters, and vests are popular knitted clothes.

The argyle pattern was adapted from the tartan used by the Scottish Clan of Campbell.

# Bb Batik Butterfly

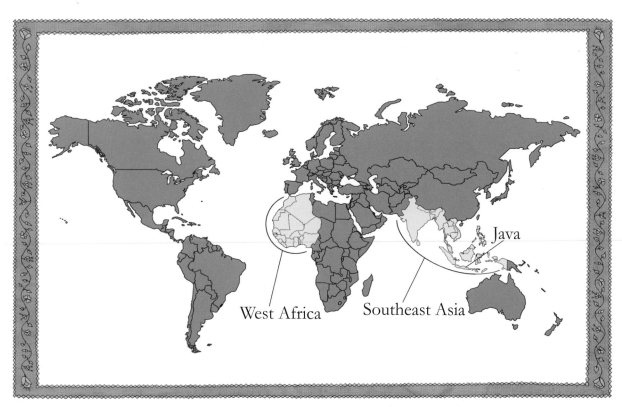

West Africa

Southeast Asia

Java

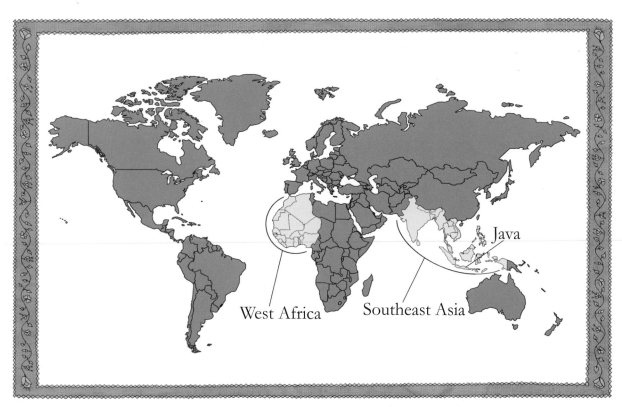 Batik is a process used to create designs on fabric. First the pattern is drawn on the cloth. Hot liquid wax is applied to areas that are *not* going to be colored, and then the fabric is dyed. This is repeated for each color.

Java is especially well known for finely detailed batiks. Batiking is also practiced throughout the rest of Southeast Asia and West Africa.

# Cc Chintz Camel

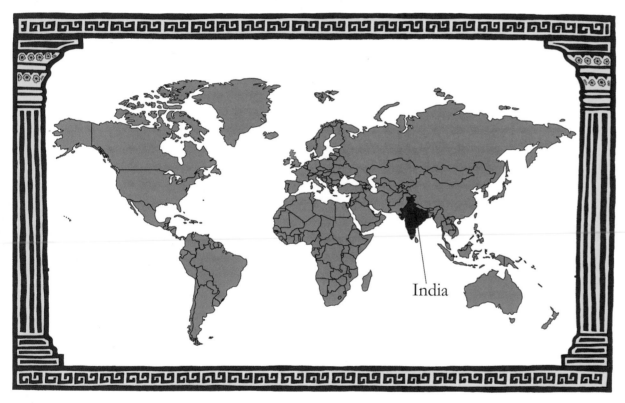

India

Chintz refers to cotton fabric printed or painted with flowers, figures, or geometric designs in five colors or more.

This fabric originated in India. In Hindi, a language spoken in India, chintz means *variegated*, or *multicolored*.

# Dd Dogs in Barkcloth

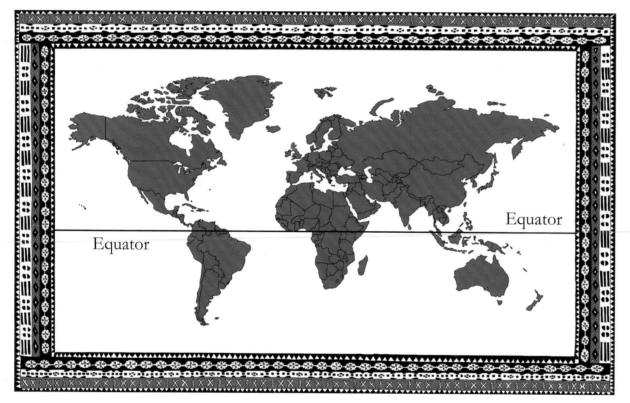

Equator

Equator

Barkcloth is made by soaking and beating strips of inner tree bark, creating a strong flexible cloth similar to felt. Patterns are painted or stenciled on the bark with tree sap.

Trees with bark that can be made into cloth grow in the warm, rainy lands near the equator. From east to west, people living along the equator make barkcloth.

# Ee Egyptian Eagle

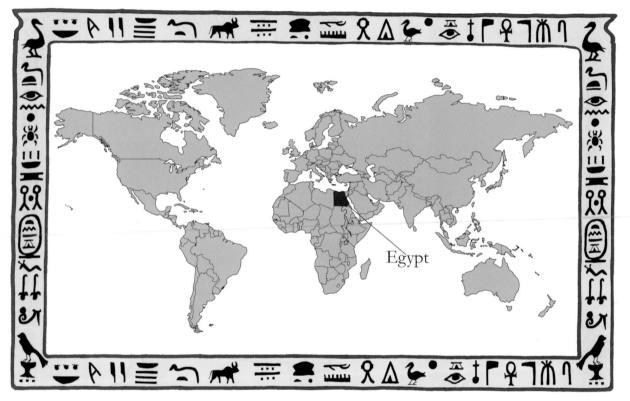

Ancient Egyptian dynasties flourished along the fertile Nile River delta of northern Africa.

Egypt

The designs here are from the tomb of Egyptian pharaoh Tutankhamun, known as King Tut. Unlike other tombs, it was never robbed; the treasures inside show us the beautiful art of the ancient Egyptians.

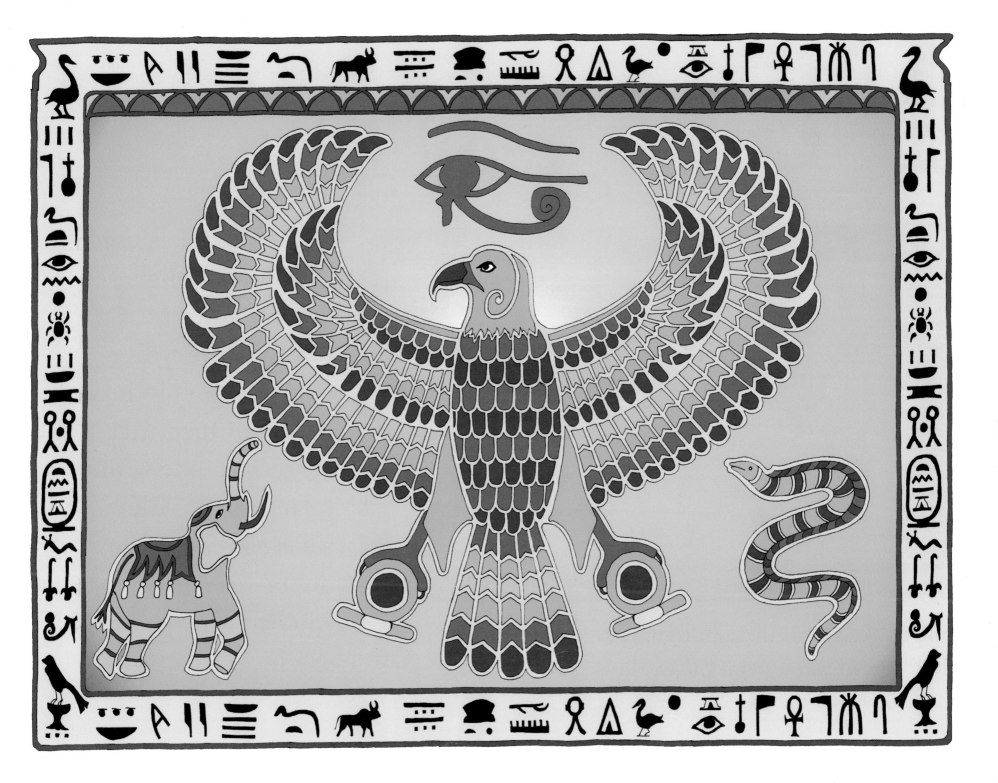

# Ff Filigree Fish

Greece

Filigree jewelry is thought to have started in Greece and then spread throughout the world.

Filigree is used in making jewelry and to decorate everything from slippers to head dresses. Open, lacy curls are made with strands of gold or silver wire. Filigree designs are also stitched onto fabric.

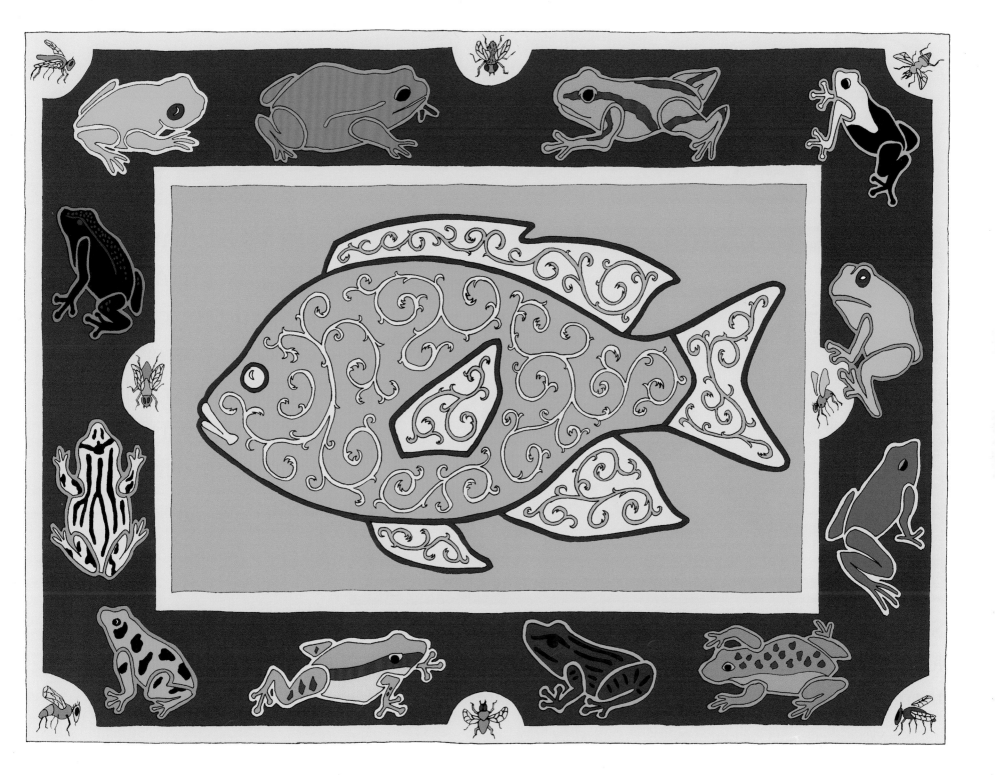

# Gg Gingham Goose

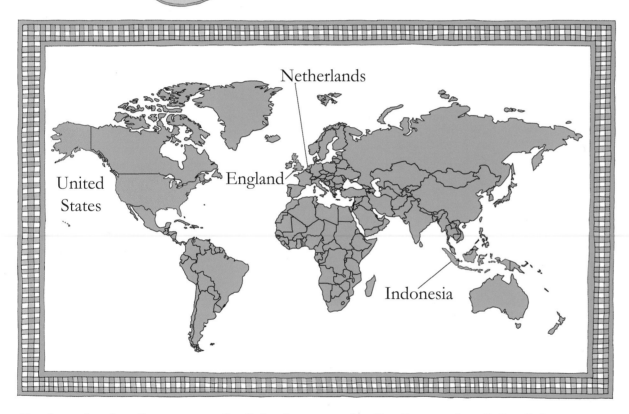

Netherlands

United
States

England

Indonesia

Gingham began as a hand-woven striped fabric. The checked pattern for gingham started when the fabric was woven by machine in textile mills.

Striped gingham probably began in Indonesia. Machine looming in textile mills began in the Netherlands and was then exported to England and the United States.

# Hh Hopi Hummingbird

Hopi designs are hand painted on pottery with brushes made of yucca leaves. Jewelry, baskets, and dolls are also made with Hopi patterns. Traditional designs are taught to each new generation.

The Hopi people live on mesas in the high desert of the American Southwest. Their name means *peaceful ones*.

# Ii Inca Iguana

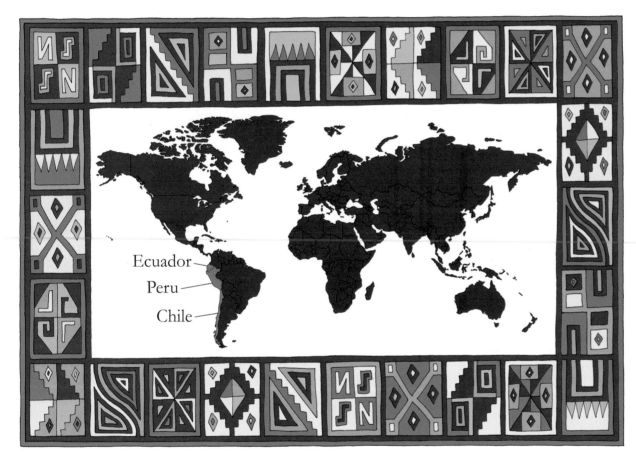

Ecuador
Peru
Chile

The Incan people used the wool of llamas and alpacas to weave ponchos with beautiful geometric designs. Sometimes they used feathers to make their ponchos.

The Inca empire was located in the Andes Mountains of what are now Ecuador, Peru, and Chile.

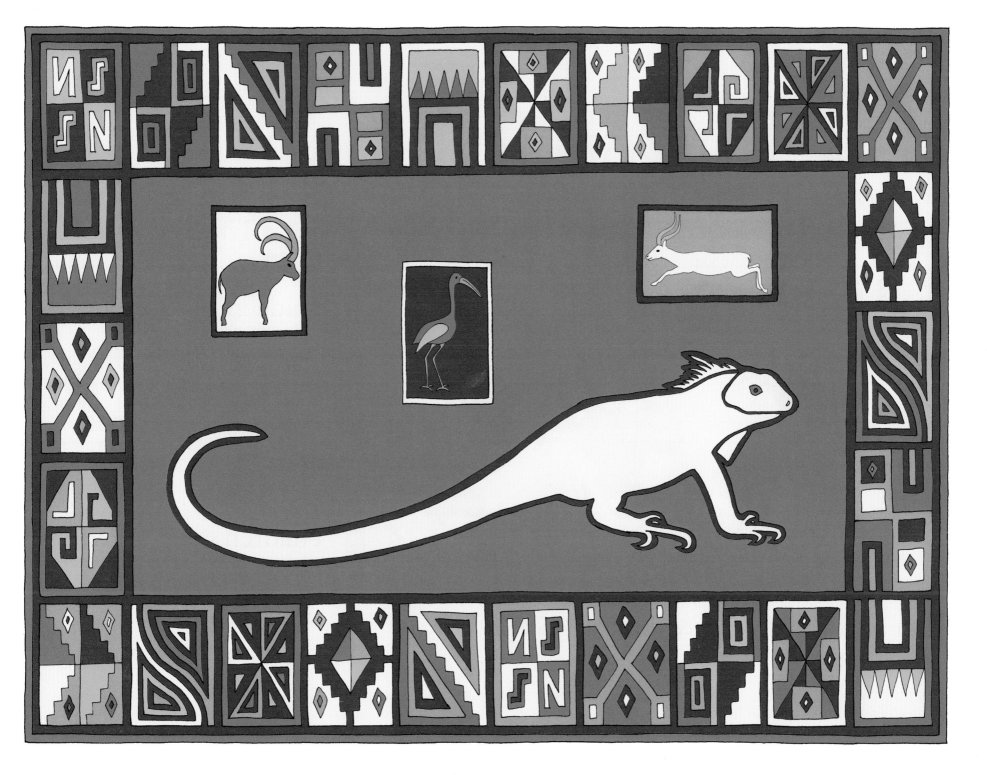

# Jj Jigsaw Jellyfish

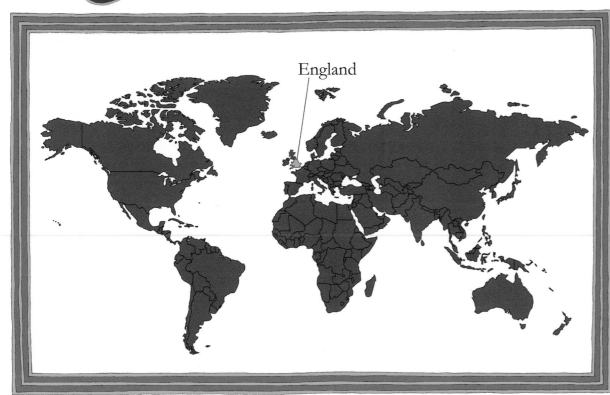

England

The mapmaker who created the first jigsaw puzzle lived in England.

The first jigsaw puzzle was made in 1767 by a mapmaker. Each piece was cut on country borderlines, and the puzzle was used to teach children geography. The early puzzles didn't interlock, so if bumped they came apart easily.

# Kk Kente Cloth King Cobra

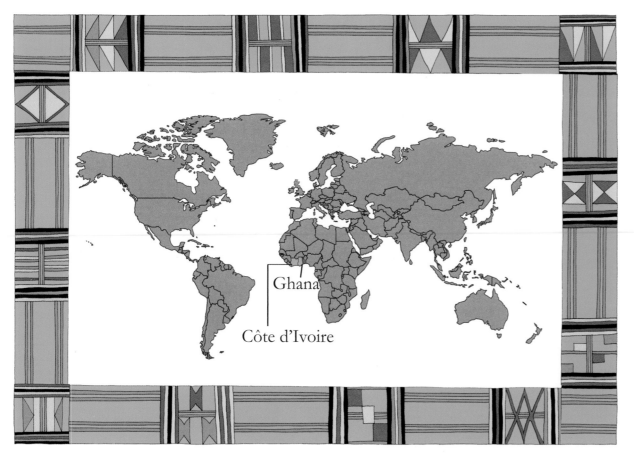

Ghana

Côte d'Ivoire

The Asanti and Ewe people weave kente cloth in long strips from three to five inches wide. The strips are sewn together and used for clothing. Each color and pattern has a particular meaning. Kente cloth was first worn by royalty.

Ghana, on the northwest coast of Africa, is the home of the Asanti and Ewe. Some Asanti live in Côte d'Ivoire (Ivory Coast).

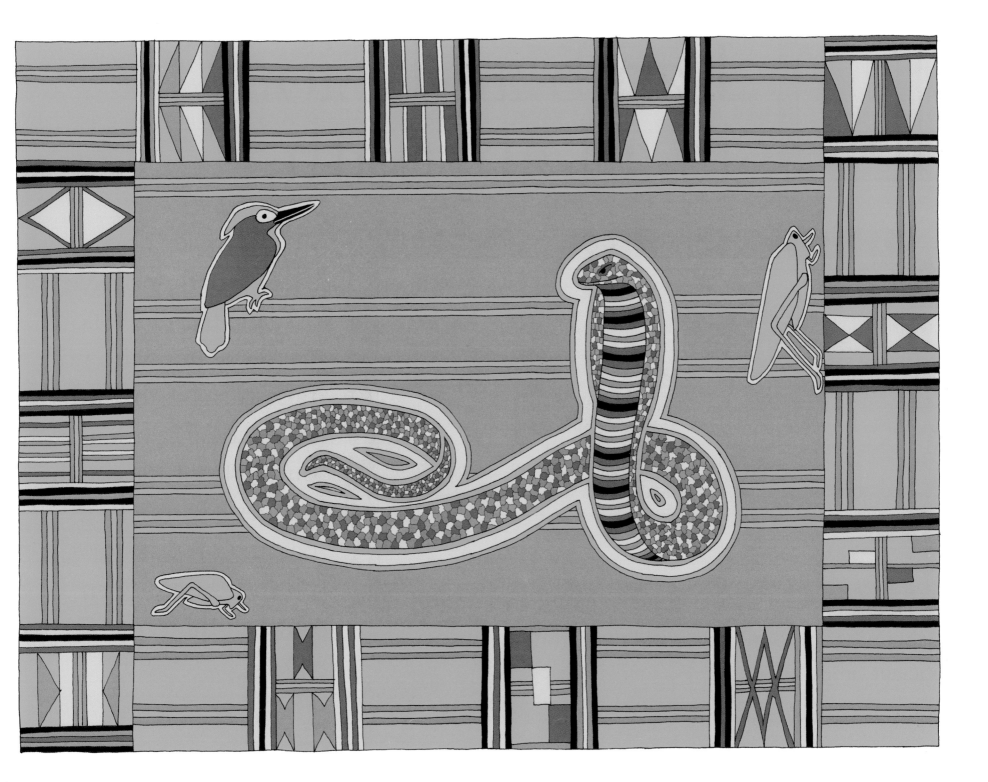

# L1 Lamb and Lion in a Labyrinth

Unlike a maze, labyrinths have a single path to follow to the center, with no false turns. Labyrinths are made in gardens, out of floor tiles, with hedges or stones, painted on walls or pottery, or are sewn onto clothing.

Labyrinths are found the world over from the most ancient times.

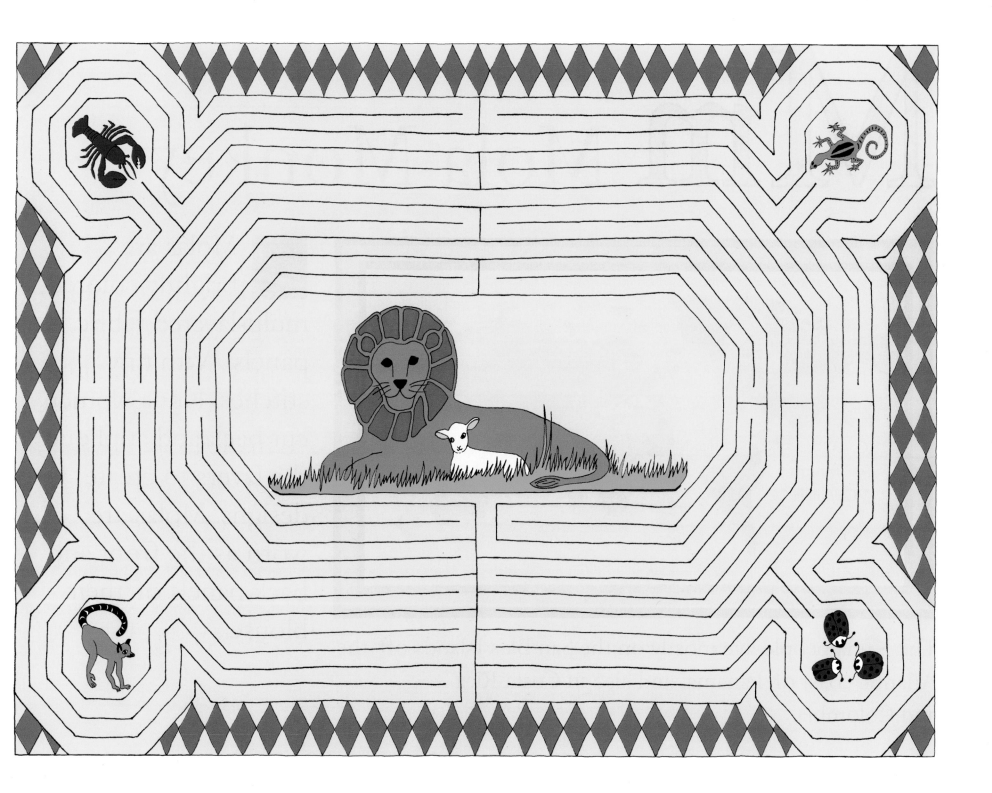

# Mm Mola Monkey

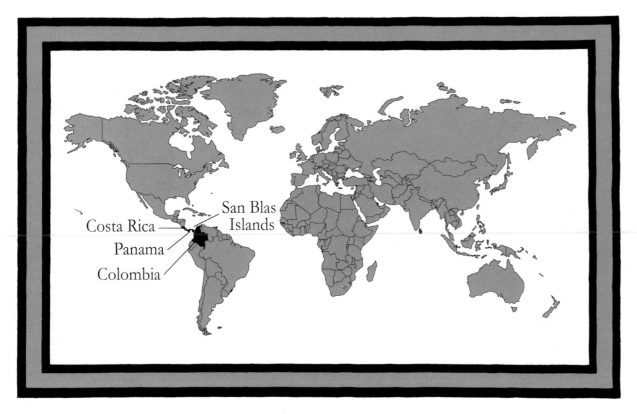

Molas are brightly colored, multi-layered fabric panels. With tiny stitches, Kuna women cut back and appliqué the layers to create designs. Molas are worn as the front and back panels of their blouse.

The Kuna people live mostly on the San Blas Islands off the Atlantic coast of Panama, and also in Costa Rica and Colombia.

# Nn Northwest Coast Nightingale

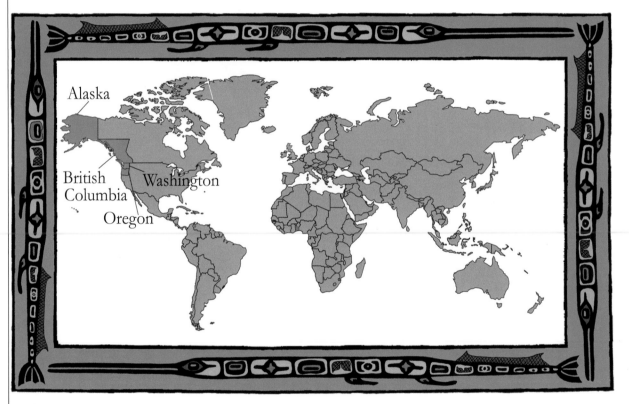

Alaska

British
Columbia

Washington

Oregon

**Northwest Coast Native** American art is mostly painted or carved wood. It portrays familiar animals using very stylized shapes. Totem poles are the best known example of this art.

Northwest Coast Native Americans live along the Pacific coast of the states of Alaska, Washington, and Oregon, as well as British Columbia. Because there is so much rain here the trees grow very tall.

# Oo Op Art Octopus

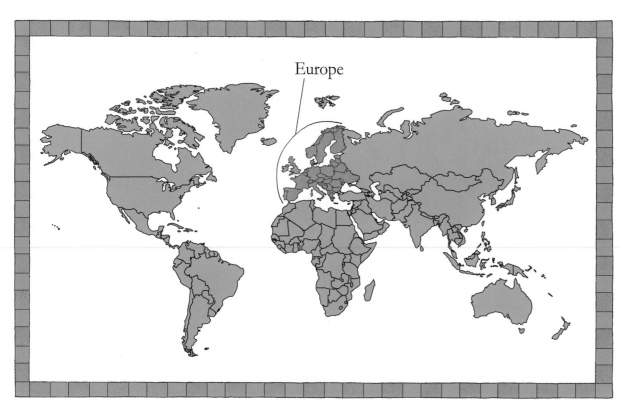

Europe

Op Art became popular in the 1960s. It is a type of optical illusion created by using shapes and colors to produce the sensation of movement called "visual vibration."

Op Art, as a school of art, had its start in Europe. But you can find Op Art patterns in indigenous art from around the world, some of which dates from ancient times.

# Pp Paisley Pig

Scotland

India

Iraq (ancient Babylon)

The paisley design is very old. Its curved teardrop shape represents a seed from the Tree of Life. It is used in paintings, for decorating buildings, in textiles, and woven into rugs.

Paisley designs were first used in ancient Babylon, which is now Iraq. More recently, paisley shawls were hand woven in India, then machine loomed in Paisley, Scotland, which is how it got its name.

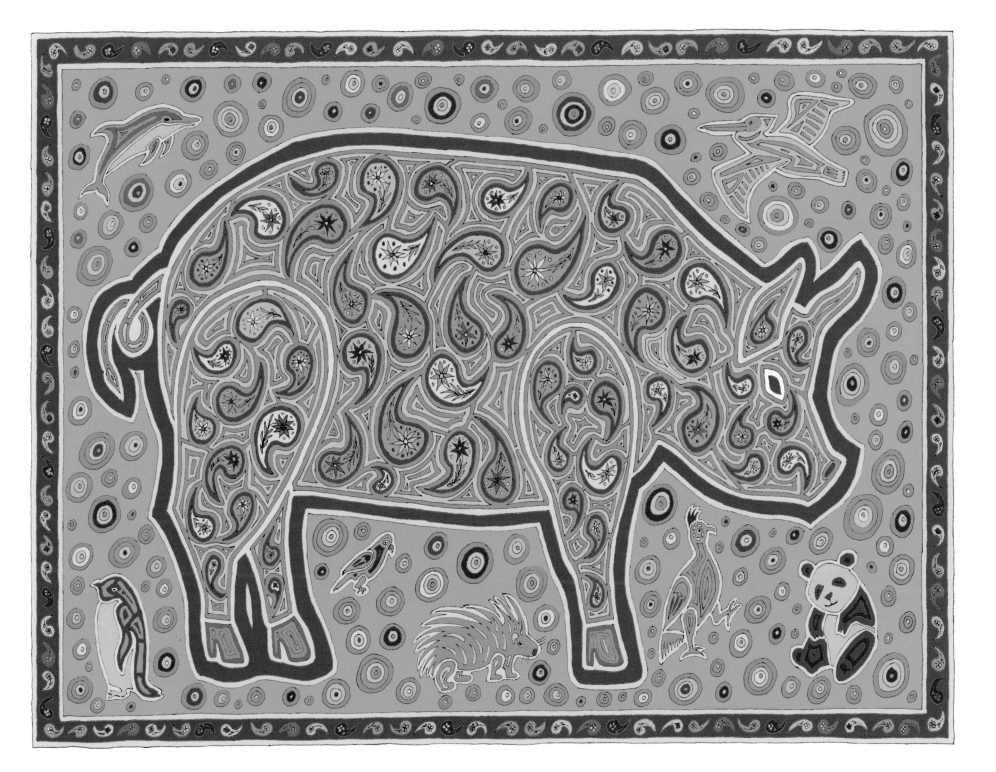

# Qq Quails in a Quatrefoil

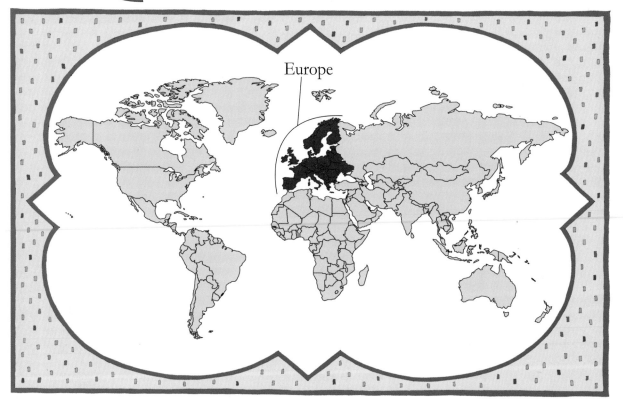

Europe

The quatrefoil represents a four-petal flower or leaf, like the four-leaf clover. Carvings in wood or stone, stained glass windows, and paintings can be found inside a quatrefoil.

Quatrefoils are most commonly used in gothic architecture, especially cathedrals and churches in Europe.

# Rr Rose Window Rabbit

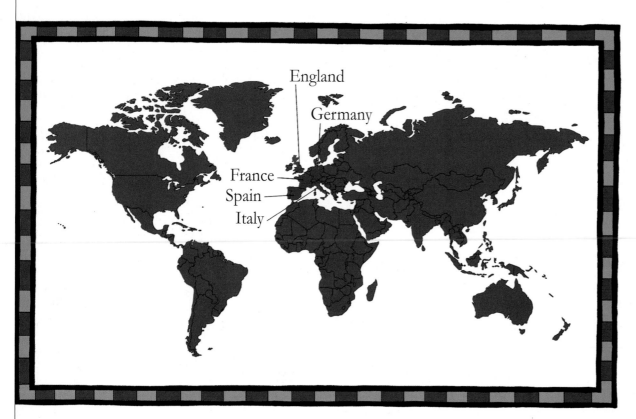

England
Germany
France
Spain
Italy

The use of rose windows started in France and spread to England, Italy, Spain, Germany, and beyond.

Rose windows are another feature found in cathedrals and churches. Early church walls were often painted with circular designs. As construction methods improved, windows were inserted and later made with stained glass.

# Ss Scrimshaw Sea Creatures

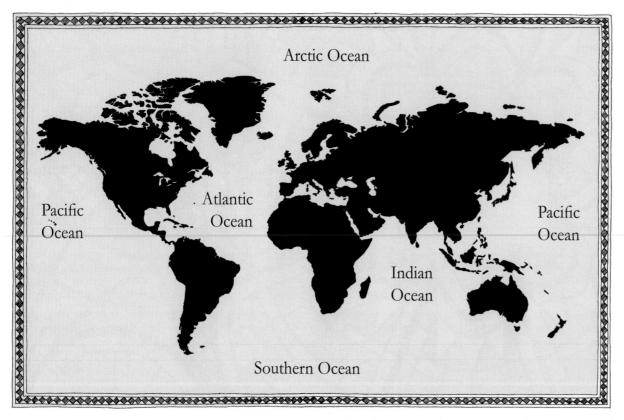

Arctic Ocean

Pacific Ocean

Atlantic Ocean

Pacific Ocean

Indian Ocean

Southern Ocean

Whaling ships sailed all the world's oceans in the nineteenth century.

Scrimshaw is the art of carving and engraving on whale teeth and bones. It's called the "folk art of American whalers." To protect whales, scrimshaw is now made using wood, nuts, or shells.

# Tt Tile Tiger

 Tile-making is an ancient art. At first, tiles were hand-shaped clay that was sun-dried. Later on, special molds, kilns, and glazes were developed. Now glass, granite, porcelain, tin, ceramic, and more are used to make tiles.

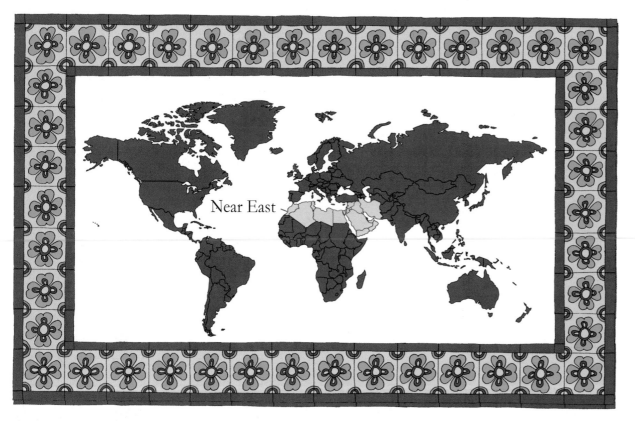

Tiles have been found in 4,000-year-old ruins in the Near East and are now used throughout the world.

# Uu Uzbeki Umbrella Birds

Wandering tribes from Uzbekistan filled their tents with hand-embroidered wall hangings like the suzani pictured here. The designs come from a mixture of traditions.

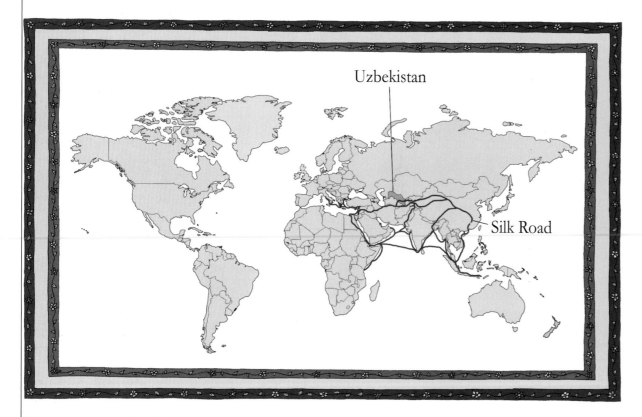

Uzbekistan

Silk Road

Due to Uzbekistan's location on the Silk Road, the cultures of China, Europe, and the Islamic world interconnected there.

# Vv Viking Vulture

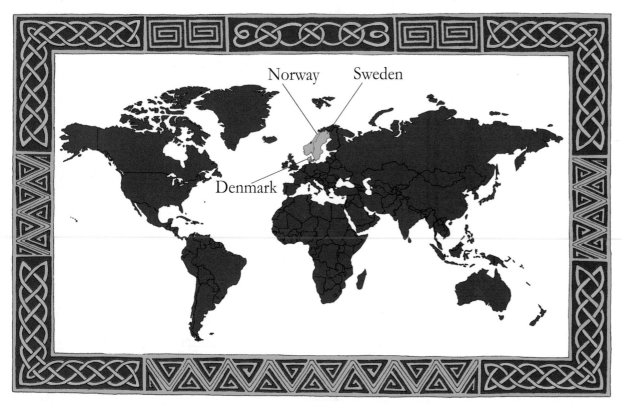

Norway   Sweden

Denmark

 The Vikings did not create art like paintings. Instead, they intricately decorated everyday objects such as swords, wagons, boats, and boxes.

The Vikings were from three of the four countries of Scandinavia, today known as Norway, Sweden, and Denmark. They traveled by ship all the way to North America and North Africa.

# Ww Willow Pattern Whale

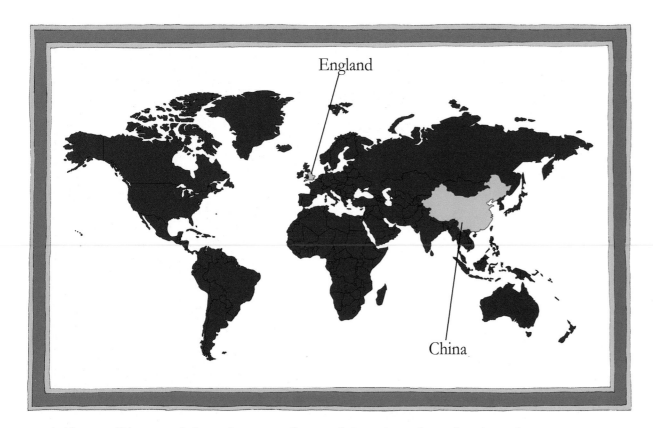

England

China

While Willow china is produced in England, the design is from China.

 The Willow Pattern is found on fine dishes, most often in shades of blue. There is a poem to go with it:

*Two birds flying high,*
*A Chinese vessel sailing by.*
*A bridge with three people,*
*sometimes four,*
*A willow tree, hanging o'er.*
*A Chinese temple, there it stands,*
*Built upon the river sands.*
*An apple tree, with apples on,*
*A crooked fence to end my song.*

—Author unknown

# Xx  X-ray-Style X-ray Fish

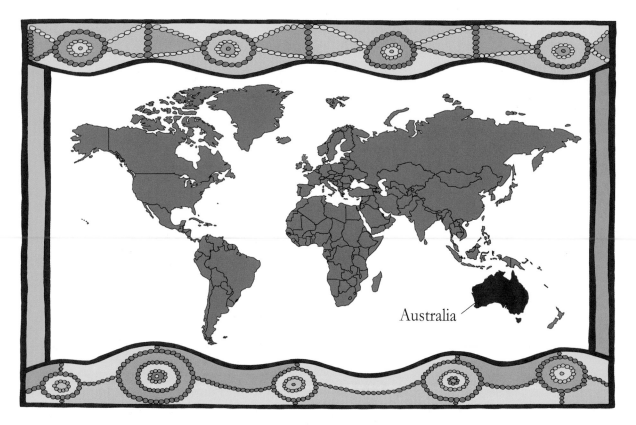

Australia

 The people of northern Australia draw in the x-ray-style. Their animal paintings show bones and internal organs just like x-rays. Forty-thousand years ago people painted this art on rock walls or on their own bodies.

Australia is an island continent and is sometimes called "Down Under."

# Yy Yarn Yak

Mexico

The Huichol people live in the mountains of north-central Mexico.

Yarn paintings are made by the Huichol people. First, a layer of beeswax is spread on a board, which is placed in the sun to soften the wax. Then designs are etched into the wax and the yarn is carefully applied.

# Zz Zulu Zebra

Zambia
Zimbabwe
Mozambique
South Africa

Zulu designs use vibrant colors and geometric patterns. They are mostly found woven into baskets or worked into bead anklets, bracelets, and necklaces.

The Zulu people live mostly in South Africa. Some Zulu live in Zambia, Zimbabwe, and Mozambique.

# Can you find all of these animals?

**A** asp    antelope    albatross    alpaca    aardvark    ant    amoeba    angel fish

**B** bugs and beetle    barracuda    beaver    bear    bee

**C** cockatoo    crane

**D** great dane    dingo    dalmation    dachshund

**E** elephant    eel

**F** frogs    flies

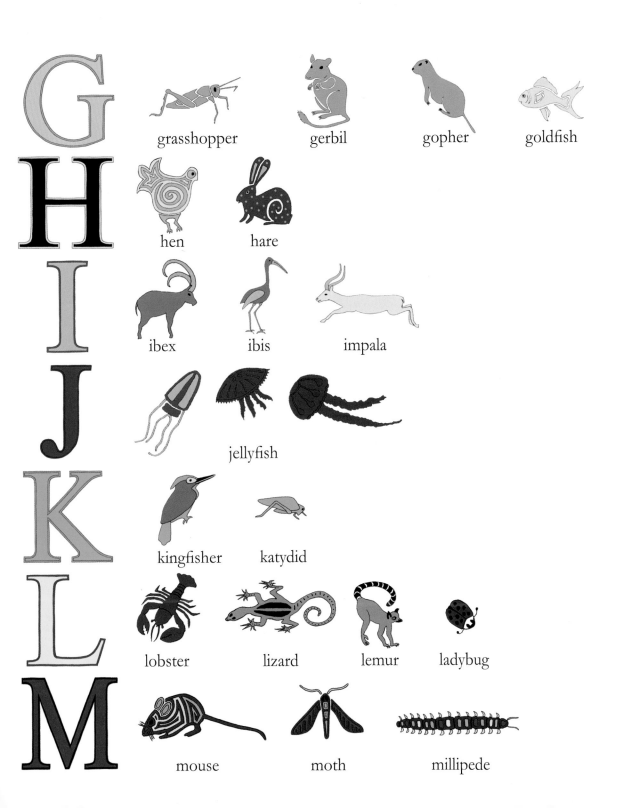

G

grasshopper    gerbil    gopher    goldfish

H

hen    hare

I

ibex    ibis    impala

J

jellyfish

K

kingfisher    katydid

L

lobster    lizard    lemur    ladybug

M

mouse    moth    millipede

# N O P Q R S T

**nurse shark**  **needle fish**

**octopus**

**porpoise**  **pelican**  **panda**  **partridge**  **porcupine**  **parrot**  **penguin**

**quetzal**  **quahog**

**rattlesnake**  **raccoon**  **rhinoceros**  **roadrunner**

**starfish**  **seahorse**  **squid**  **swordfish**  **sand dollar**  **scallop**  **sharks**

**turkey**  **tapir**  **tarantula**  **tortoise**  **toucan**  **trout**  **toad**  **tick**

U

unicorn fish

V

vicuna    viper    vole    vampire bat

W

walrus    wolf    wasp    woodpecker    wombat    worm

X

x-ray fish

Y

yellow-billed hornbill    yellow-tailed damselfish    yellowjacket

Z

zorilla    zebra-tailed lizard    zebra fish

# Can you find these colors?

apple red

blue

canary yellow

crimson

dark brown

dun

fuchsia

forest green

grass green

gold

indigo

ivory

jade

kelly green

lavender

lemon

maroon

olive

orange

pink

purple

quince

rose

ruby

sand

teal

terra cotta

ultramarine

violet

yellow

# Pronunciation Guide

**Argyle**: [**ahr**-gahyl]

**Batik**: [**buh**-teek]

**Chintz**: [chints]

**Filigree**: [**fil**-i-gree]

**Gingham**: [**ging**-uhm]

**Hopi**: [**hoh**-pee]

**Huichol**: [we-**chohl**]

**Iguana**: [i-**gwah**-nuh]

**Inca**: [**ing**-kuh]

**Jigsaw**: [**jig**-saw]

**Kente**: [**ken**-tey]

**Labyrinth**: [**lab**-uh-rinth]

**Mola**: [**moh**-luh]

**Quatrefoil**: [**kat**-er-foil, **ka**-truh-foil]

**Scrimshaw**: [**skrim**-shaw]

**Tutankhamun**: [toot-ahng-**kah**-muhn, toot-eng-**kah**-muhn]

**Uzbeki**: [**uhz**-bek-ee]

**Vulture**: [**vuhl**-cher]

**Zulu**: [**zoo**-loo]